THE JEWELLERY SHOP ROBBERY

Carmel Reilly
Kate Ashforth

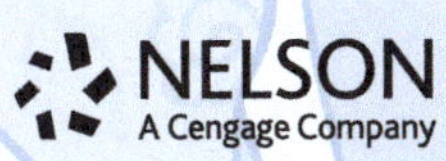

Australia • Brazil • Japan • Korea • Mexico • Singapore • Spain • United Kingdom • United States

The Jewellery Shop Robbery

Fast Forward
Yellow Level 8

Text: Carmel Reilly
Illustrations: Kate Ashforth
Editor: Johanna Rohan
Design: Vonda Pestana
Series design: James Lowe
Production controller: Hanako Smith
Audio recordings: Juliet Hill, Picture Start
Spoken by: Matthew King and Abbe Holmes
Reprint: Jennifer Foo

Text © 2007 Cengage Learning Australia Pty Limited
Illustrations © 2007 Cengage Learning Australia Pty Limited

Copyright Notice
This Work is copyright. No part of this Work may be reproduced, stored in a retrieval system, or transmitted in any form or by any means without prior written permission of the Publisher. Except as permitted under the Copyright Act 1968, for example any fair dealing for the purposes of private study, research, criticism or review, subject to certain limitations. These limitations include: Restricting the copying to a maximum of one chapter or 10% of this book, whichever is greater; Providing an appropriate notice and warning with the copies of the Work disseminated; Taking all reasonable steps to limit access to these copies to people authorised to receive these copies; Ensuring you hold the appropriate Licences issued by the Copyright Agency Limited ("CAL"), supply a remuneration notice to CAL and pay any required fees.

ISBN 978 0 17 012516 1
ISBN 978 0 17 012513 0 (set)

Cengage Learning Australia
Level 7, 80 Dorcas Street
South Melbourne, Victoria Australia 3205
Phone: 1300 790 853

Cengage Learning New Zealand
Unit 4B Rosedale Office Park
331 Rosedale Road, Albany, North Shore NZ 0632
Phone: 0508 635 766

For learning solutions, visit **cengage.com.au**

Printed in Australia by Ligare Pty Ltd
9 10 11 12 13 14 15 22 21 20 19 18

Evaluated in independent research by staff from the Department of Language, Literacy and Arts Education at the University of Melbourne.

Contents

Chapter 1

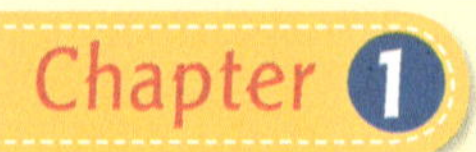

The Jewellery Shop Robbery

One day, Eddie was walking home from school.
As he came around a corner, he saw a lot of people outside the jewellery shop.

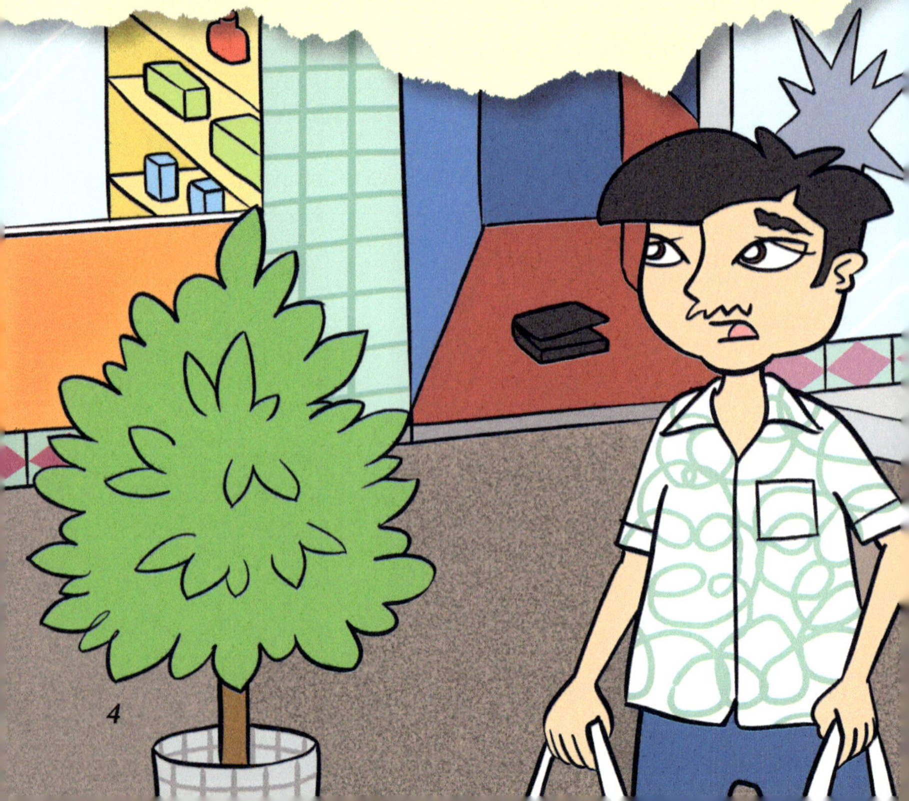

"What's going on?"
he said to a woman
standing next to him.

"The jewellery shop has been robbed,"
she said.
"The robbers took all the jewellery."

That night, the jewellery shop robbery was on the TV news. The reporter said that people on the street had seen the men get away in a red car.

"When I came home from school, I saw a red car parked outside the empty house next door," Eddie said to his mum.

Mum smiled. "Oh, there are lots of red cars around," she said.

"But I have not seen this one here before," Eddie said.

Running Words 126

Chapter 2

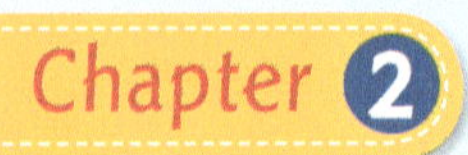

The Red Car

After dinner, Eddie went outside.
He looked over at the house next door.
It was dark and empty.
He looked out at the street.
The red car was still parked there.

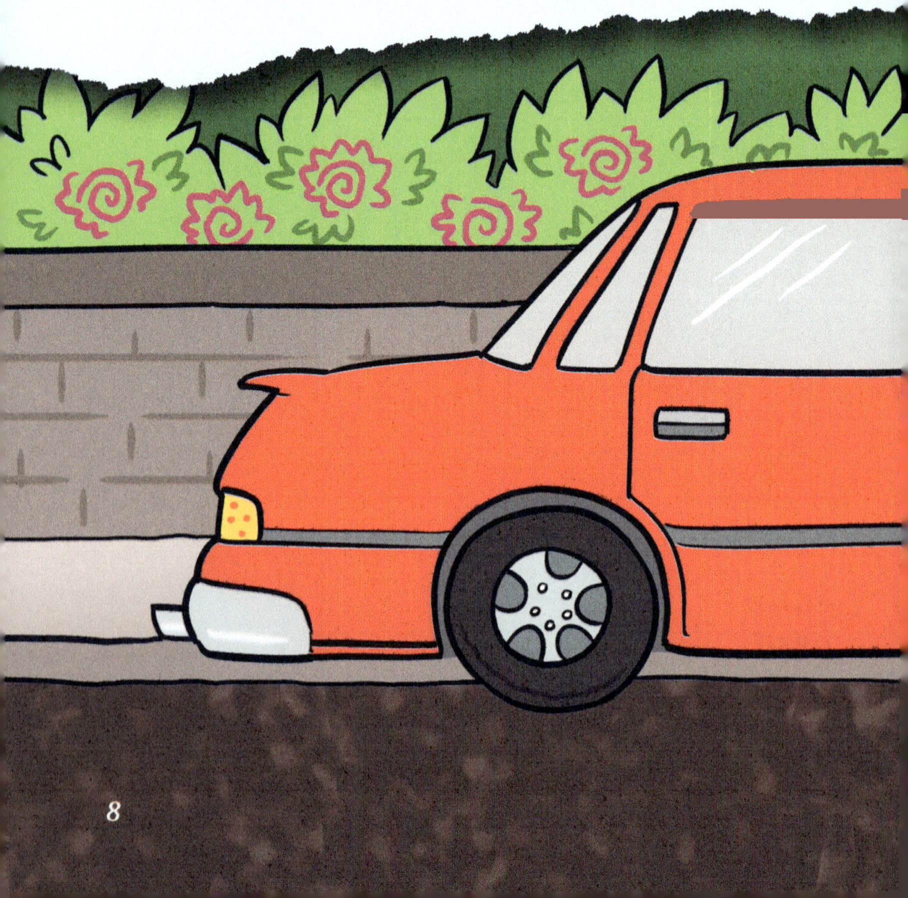

Eddie walked over to the car
and looked inside.
Just then, there was a noise
from somewhere behind him.

Eddie turned around.
The noise was coming
from the empty house.
He had to go and have a look.

He walked up the path
and went around the back of the house.

Eddie walked up to a window
and looked in.
He could not believe what he saw.

Chapter 3

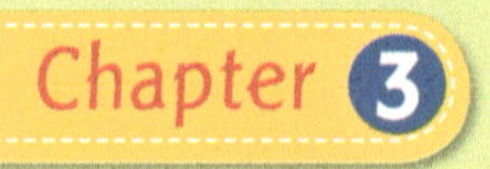

What's Going On?

Eddie saw two men sitting at a table.
They were taking things
out of a big black box.
Eddie could see that it was jewellery.

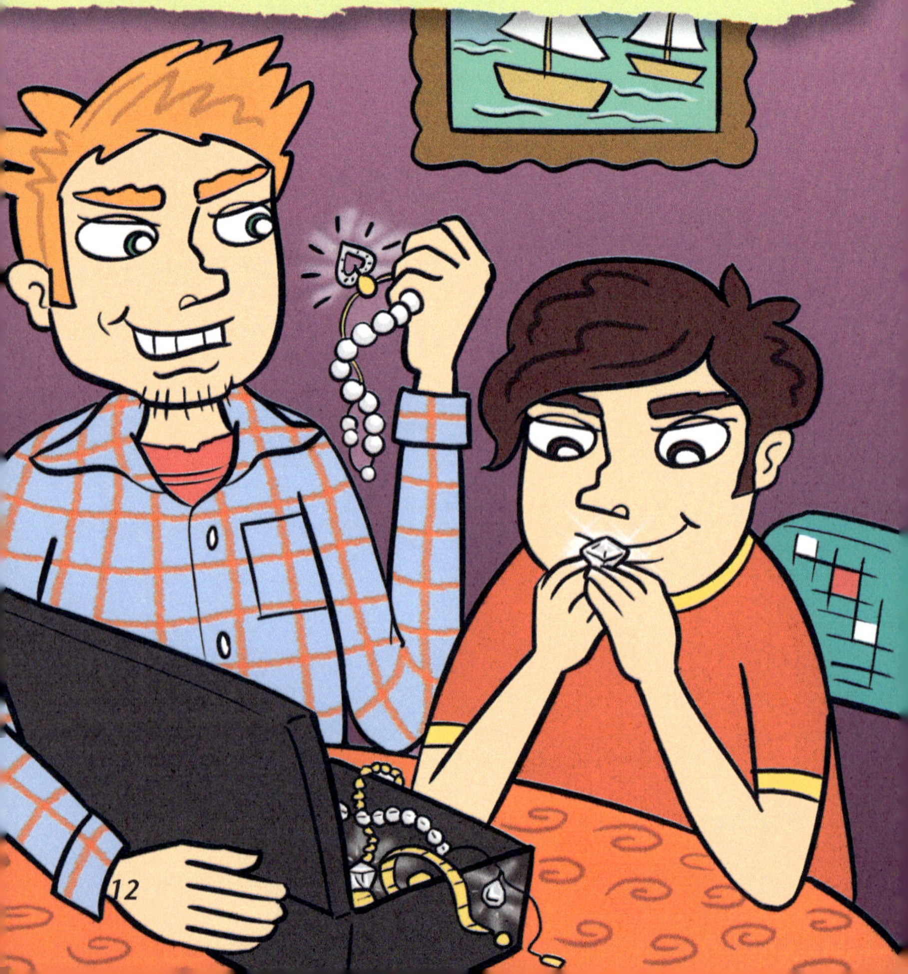

Eddie moved away from the window.
He ran down the path
and into his house.

"Mum, Mum! Call the police! The jewellery robbers are next door," he said.

"Oh, come on, Eddie!" said Mum.

"Really, Mum! Go and have a look if you don't believe me," he said.

Mum looked hard at Eddie.
She could see that he was not making it up.
So, she called the police.

The police came to the house.
"Very good work, Eddie,"
said one of the police
as they took the robbers away.
"You're going to make
a good detective one day."

"I think I am, too," Eddie said.